ALL-STAR SPORTS PUZZLES

Hockey

GAMES, TRIVIA, QUIZZES AND MORE!

Jesse Ross

RAINCOAST BOOKS
www.raincoast.com

Thanks to my family for always supporting me,
and to all my friends who helped along the way.

Raincoast Books gratefully acknowledges the financial support of the Province of British Columbia through the BC Arts Council and the Book Publishing Tax Credit and the Government of Canada through the Canada Council for the Arts, and the Book Publishing Industry Development Program (BPIDP).

Edited by Brian Scrivener
Cover design by Teresa Bubela
Interior design by Warren Clark

Library and Archives Canada Cataloguing in Publication

Ross, Jesse, 1986-
    All-star sports puzzles : hockey / Jesse Paul Ross.

    ISBN 13: 978-1-55192-810-4
    ISBN 10: 1-55192-810-8

    1. Puzzles—Juvenile literature. 2. Hockey—Miscellanea—Juvenile literature. I. Title.

GV1493.R655 2007   j793.73   C2007-900490-3

Library of Congress Control Number: 2007921215

Raincoast Books
9050 Shaughnessy Street
Vancouver, British Columbia
Canada V6P 6E5
www.raincoast.com

In the United States:
Publishers Group West
1700 Fourth Street
Berkeley, California
94710

Raincoast Books is committed to protecting the environment and to the responsible use of natural resources. We are working with suppliers and printers to phase out our use of paper produced from ancient forests. This book is printed with vegetable-based inks on 100% ancient-forest-free, 40% post-consumer recycled, processed chlorine- and acid-free paper. For further information, visit our website at www.raincoast.com/publishing/

Printed in Canada by Webcom

10 9 8 7 6 5 4 3 2 1

CONTENTS

Matching

Trivia

Fill Me In

Puzzles

Long Puzzles

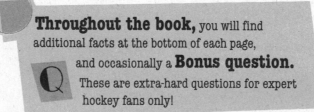

Throughout the book, you will find additional facts at the bottom of each page, and occasionally a **Bonus question.** These are extra-hard questions for expert hockey fans only!

Check out our website at **www.allstarsportspuzzles.com**

Note: All puzzles are accurate, to the best of our knowledge, as of September 2007.

The World's Game

Match these hockey stars with their native country.
Watch out, the USA and Canada both have two players on the list.

Roberto Luongo	Sweden
Brian Rafalski	Finland
Fredrik Modin	Canada
Pavel Datsyuk	Kazakhstan
Milan Hejduk	USA
Katie King	Germany
Marco Sturm	Russia
Sandis Ozolinsh	Canada
Marian Gaborik	Switzerland
David Aebischer	Czech Republic
Nikolai Antropov	Latvia
Sarah Vaillancourt	USA
Miikka Kiprusoff	Slovakia

In 2002, Swede Nicklas Lidstrom became the first non-North American player to win the Conn Smythe trophy for playoff MVP since the award was first given in 1965.

Beginner's Luck

The last names of 16 recent Rookie of the Year winners are hidden below. They are written forwards or backwards, and are hidden diagonally, horizontally and vertically. After you have crossed out each name, the leftover letters spell out the only team whose players have won the Rookie of the Year trophy three years in a row.

T	R	S	A	M	S	O	N	O	V
N	U	R	E	T	U	S	V	R	O
H	O	D	R	A	R	E	B	A	K
E	F	S	R	O	C	N	T	Y	V
A	L	O	S	H	M	H	D	C	O
T	E	A	K	D	C	N	P	R	K
L	B	I	R	T	E	L	E	O	O
E	N	U	E	W	G	R	L	F	B
Y	R	E	U	O	E	A	F	T	A
Y	L	E	M	I	E	U	X	L	N
F	I	E	N	N	A	L	E	S	A
N	Z	J	A	C	K	M	A	N	S

Names

Daniel ALFREDSSON
Ed BELFOUR
Bryan BERARD
Chris DRURY
Scott GOMEZ
Dany HEATLEY
Barret JACKMAN
Brian LEETCH

Mario LEMIEUX
Evgeni NABOKOV
Joe NIEUWENDYK
Alexander OVECHKIN
Andrew RAYCROFT
Sergei SAMSONOV
Teemu SELANNE
Gary SUTER

In his rookie year (1992-93), Teemu Selanne had an amazing 132 points, scoring 76 goals. Since then, no one in the league has scored more than 69 goals.

Team with three straight Rookies of the Year (in 1944, '45 and '46): _____

Famous Firsts

Can you figure out what these players were the first ever to do?

1) Manon Rheaume was the first ...

A) Fan to win one million dollars during an intermission contest.
B) Female referee in the NHL.
C) Woman to play in the NHL.
D) Person to sue the NHL, because her son was not selected during the entry draft.

2) On December 6, 2005, Miikka Kiprusoff became the first goalie in NHL history to ...

A) Get three points in one game (three assists).
B) Play an entire game, earn a shutout and lose, all in one night.
C) Play a shift in another position. (He was pulled with a minute left, and laced up during a TV time-out to play as a forward.)
D) Not wear a glove. The eccentric goalie played the game with two blockers, one on each hand.

3) Mario Lemieux is the first person to ...

A) Own and play for the same team, at the same time.
B) Score a hat trick in three consecutive games.
C) Send his Stanley Cup ring back to the jeweller. The reason? It didn't fit on any of his fingers!
D) Return from retirement ... four times.

4) Mats Sundin is the first European player to ...

A) Publicly state he wants the NHL to expand to Europe, making it a "World Hockey League."
B) Win Don Cherry's "Bulldog of the Year" award, for hardest-working player in the league.
C) Captain an NHL team.
D) Be drafted first overall in the NHL Entry Draft, in 1989.

5) In 2005-06, the longest current streak of any pro sports team ended when this team missed the playoffs, for the first time since 1979. Which team was it?

A) Toronto Maple Leafs
B) St. Louis Blues
C) Dallas Stars
D) Boston Bruins

6) What happened for the first time ever at a major women's tournament at the 2006 Winter Olympics?

A) Canada did not play the USA in the final (Canada played Sweden for gold).
B) No team lost by more than five goals.
C) More people watched the women's final than the men's final.
D) There was a fight. American Krissy Wendell dropped the gloves with Kavolina Rantamaki of Finland in their quarterfinal game.

Wayne Gretzky holds or shares an amazing 60 NHL records.

7) What happened for the first time ever in a Stanley Cup Final, on June 5th, 2006?

A) A player (Chris Pronger) scored on a penalty shot.

B) Neither team (Edmonton or Carolina) registered a shot in the second period.

C) The national anthem of Canada was not completed because the singer, Mariah Carey, could not remember the lyrics.

D) The game was not played in either team's arena. (Scheduled for Raleigh, North Carolina, the game had to be moved to Nashville, Tennessee because of weather issues.)

8) What happened for the first time ever on February 25th, 1940?

A) The president of the United States, Franklin D. Roosevelt, entertained the Stanley Cup winning Boston Bruins at the White House.

B) Due to a shortage of players in the league, clubs were allowed to dress players who were not under contract. (The Red Wings' janitor played defense for five games.)

C) The NHL introduced the offside rule.

D) An NHL game was broadcast on TV. (Rangers beat the Canadiens, 6-2.)

9) After the lockout, much was made of the "New NHL" going into the 2005-06 season. What happened for the first time ever that year?

A) There were more minor penalties (18,450) than the last two seasons combined. (2002-03 & 2003-04 had 16,954 total minors.)

B) Two rookies, Alexander Ovechkin and Sidney Crosby, both recorded over 100 points.

C) Every game was a sellout.

D) No player received more than 10 fighting majors.

The Stanley Cup has been to the Czech Republic, Sweden, Russia, Finland, Japan, Switzerland, the Bahamas and the White House.

Dream Teams

Can you spot the three made-up teams mixed in with this list of now-defunct NHL squads?

Montreal Maroons

Winnipeg Winners

Oakland Seals

Colorado Rockies

Pittsburgh Pirates

Buffalo Buffaloes

Kansas City Cavaliers

New York Americans

Hamilton Tigers

Hartford Whalers

 What is the record for most losses in a season?
Which team holds this infamous record?

Lost Letters

Fill in the missing letter in the middle to complete the last letter of the player's name on the left, and the first letter of the name on the right. The missing letters, taken from top to bottom, spell out the name of the first player to receive both the Calder and Vezina trophies in the same year.

Steve Poaps	___	odd Marchant
Carlo Colaiacov	___	laf Kolzig
Joe Thornto	___	icklas Lidstrom
Chris Drur	___	an Stastny
Gilbert Brul	___	rik Cole
Andrej Meszaro	___	ean O'Donnell
Wayne Van Dor	___	avel Vorobiev
Marty Turc	___	le-Kristian Tollefsen
Brad Boye	___	ami Salo
Matthew Lombard	___	an Moran
Martin Era	___	om Poti
Mike Ribeir	___	ssi Vaananen

First player to win the Calder and Vezina trophies in the same year:

_____

Talk about passing the torch! The year Wayne Gretzky retired, Jaromir Jagr was in on 52.5 percent of Pittsburgh Penguins' goals (either scoring or assisting on them).

The (Inter) National Hockey League

Try to place these 10 countries in the correct order, corresponding to the number of players from each country in the NHL in 2006-07. #1 is the most, #2 the second most, and so on. Be warned, this is one of the hardest puzzles in the book!

Canada   Russia   USA   Slovakia   Switzerland

Czech Republic   Ukraine   Germany   Finland   Sweden

#1) _____

#2) _____

#3) _____

#4) _____

#5) _____

#6) _____

#7) _____

#8) _____

#9) _____

#10) _____

Darryl Sittler holds the record for most points in one game with 10 — 6 goals and 4 assists against the Bruins. Dave Reece, the Boston goalie, never played another NHL game.

Game Day Crozzle

Fill in the crossword grid by answering each clue, corresponding to the number in the grid.

Across

1) After Overtime.
5) Odd - _____ Rush.
8) Type of penalty that has an automatic ejection.
9) Always two of these on the ice.
11) Phil Kessel's country.
13) Luc Robitaille is the highest scoring one of these in NHL history.
15) Wayne Gretzky was traded to the L.A. Kings for a couple of players, a couple of draft picks, and a whole lot of this.
16) _____ - Net.
18) Games can no longer end this way.
19) ___ - Captain.
20) Retired Edmonton forward Jari _____
21) "Miracle On _____"

Down

2) Hockey _____ of Fame.
3) This team won the cup in '84, '85, '87, '88 & '90.
4) Each coach can use this once per game.
5) _____ Sundin.
6) National Women's Hockey League, abbreviation.
7) Redirection.
9) Hit.
10) Brett Hull's relationship to Bobby Hull.
11) When the underdog team wins.
12) First name of retired defensemen MacInnis and Iafrate.
14) Two of these dress for each game.
16) __ Jovanovski.
17) This is shot around 50 times a game.

How's this for irony? Russ Blinco was the first player to appear in a game wearing glasses.

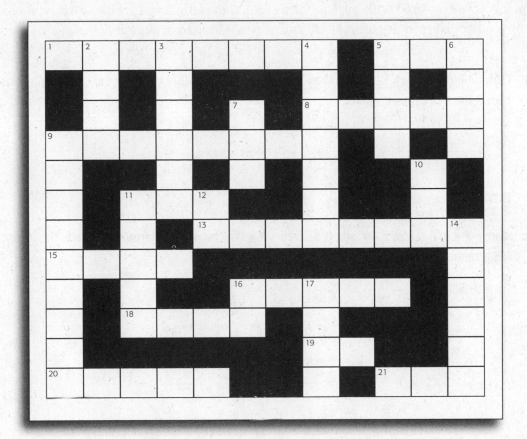

 The Maurice "Rocket" Richard trophy was introduced to the NHL in 1998. Through to 2006, the award has been handed out to the top goal-scorer seven times. Can you name all the winners? Hint: there was a three-way tie in 2004.

Fill Me In

Fill in the answers by using the letters in the box below. Cross out each letter as you go. When you've answered both questions, the remaining letters will spell out the name of the player in question #1 – but first you'll have to unscramble them.
We've started you off by filling in a few letters.

1. **Only one player in NHL history has recorded every possible type of goal in a single game. Name the five types of goals.**

A) _E_ __ __ __   __ __ __ __ __ _G_ __ __

B) __ __ _W_ __ __   __ __ __ _Y_

C) _S_ __ __ __ __ __ - _H_ __ __ __ __ __

D) __ __ _N_ __ __ __ __   __ __ _H_ __ __

E) __ _M_ __ __ __ __ - _N_ __ __

2. **Name the five teams who won the Stanley Cup in the new millennium, before the lockout. (One team won twice.)**

A) __ __ __ __ __ _A_ __   __ __ __ __ __ __ __ __ __ __

B) __ __ __   __ __ __ __ __ __ _Y_ __   __ __ __ __ __ __

C) __ __ __ __ __ __ __ _T_ __   __ __ __ __   __ __ __ __ __ __

D) __ __ __ __ __ __ __ __ __   _A_ __ __ __ __ __ __ __ __

E) _N_ __ __   __ __ __ __ __ __   __ __ __ _V_ __ __ __ __

```
A̶ A̶ A A A A A A A A A B C C D D D D
D D D E̶ E E E E E E E E E E E E E E
E E E E G̶ G G G H̶ H̶ H H H H H I I I I I I I
J J L L L L L L L L M̶ M M M M N̶ N̶ N̶ N
N N N N N O O O O O O O O P P P P P
R R R R R R R R S̶ S S S S S S S T̶ T
T T T T T T T U V̶ V V V W̶ W W W W X
X̶ X̶ Y Y Y Y Y
```

Unscramble the letters that remain in the box above to spell the player from Question #1

__ __ __ __ __   __ __ __ __ __ __ __

Grant Fuhr recorded 14 points in the 1983-84 season, the most ever by a goalie.

Know Your Teams

How well do you know the teams in the NHL? Try to answer all the questions below.

1) The only team with a type of politician in its name.

    _____

2) You might say it's the saddest team in the league.

    _____

3) This team is a snowboarder's worst nightmare.

    _____

4) Some would say this team is pure evil.

    _____

5) Firefighters do not like this team one bit.

    _____

6) This team can cause mass evacuations.

    _____

7) There are about 33 million people who lay claim to the name of this team.

    _____

8) This team used to be named after a Disney movie.

    _____

9) This team is named after a type of sword.

    _____

 The record for career shutouts is 103. Who holds this record? Who are second and third on the career shutout list?

What Do They Have in Common?

See if you can figure out what each of the following have in common.

1) Dave Williams, Dale Hunter and Tie Domi?

A) They rank as the top three all-time penalty minute leaders in the NHL.

B) In a *Sports Illustrated* online poll, they were voted the three ugliest players in NHL history.

C) They all appeared on the same celebrity edition of Jeopardy. Dale Hunter won first place, bringing in $32,400 for his charity.

2) The New York Islanders, the Toronto Maple Leafs and the Boston Bruins?

A) They all share the same farm team in the AHL: the Portland Marlies.

B) All three teams have their engravings misspelled on the Stanley Cup (New York Ilanders, Toronto Maple Leaes, Bqstqn Bruins).

C) They all joined the NHL in the 1950s.

3) Joe Sakic, Joe Thornton and Markus Naslund?

A) They have all captained a Cup-winning team.

B) They all wear #19.

C) At one time they were the three highest-paid players in the NHL, with a combined salary of $32,000,000.

Ice hockey first made its appearance at the 1920 Olympics in Antwerp, Belgium. The strange part is, they were the Summer Games!

4) Martin Rucinsky, Brian Rolston and Martin Straka?

A) They were all police officers before joining the NHL.

B) In 2001-02, all three took a hooking penalty in every single game of the season.

C) They have all played for three different teams during one NHL season.

5) Nick Kyprios, Kelly Hrudey and Bill Clement?

A) These three worked together during the lockout year to form the OT League (Old Timers League).

B) All three broke their legs in the same game on October 31, 1991.

C) They are all former players who are now TV commentators.

6) Henrik and Daniel Sedin?

A) A lot, they're identical twins.

B) On November 5, 2006 they both had 237 career points.

C) In the 2005-06 season, they both set career totals for goals, assists, shots, penalty minutes and power-play points.

D) All of the above.

7) Jimmy Peters Sr. and son Jimmy Peters Jr.?

A) At different times they both centred the famous Detroit line of Ted Lindsay and Gordie Howe.

B) They co-own the Columbus Blue Jackets.

C) They rank first and second on the Boston Bruins all-time penalty minute list.

8) John Madden, Jarkko Ruutu and Tomas Vokoun?

A) They have all played both goal and forward in the NHL.
B) During the lockout in 2004-05, they all played for HIFK Helsinki in Finland.
C) In the 1996 World Junior Championship, they were all captains of their respective teams (Canada, Finland and the Czech Republic).

9) Bobby Carpenter, Phil Housley and Tom Barrasso?

A) They were the three co-captains of the 1982 USA team that won Olympic Gold.
B) All three were drafted directly from high school in the first round, and played in the NHL the next year.
C) They have won more individual NHL awards than any other American-born players.
D) All of the above.

10) San Juan, Puerto Rico, Truro, Nova Scotia and London, England?

A) The NHL has played exhibition games in all three cities.
B) In 2006, the ERHL (Extreme Roller Hockey League) added teams in all three cities.
C) According to the Hockey Hall of Fame, the sport of hockey (which later became ice hockey) originated at these three locations around the same time, in the early 1850s.

In his 11-year NHL career, Clint Smith played 483 games, netting 397 points. The amazing thing is, he only registered 24 total penalty minutes. (He played three full seasons without taking a penalty!)

Round and Round

This puzzle goes in a spiral, starting with the top left corner and working around until all the spaces are filled up. The start of the next clue is formed by the last one or two letters of the previous answer. The number in parentheses at the end of each clue gives the number of letters in the answer. Try working backwards if you get stuck.

1) Commissioner of the NHL, Gary _____ (7)

2) One of the three California-based NHL teams. (7)

3) Any two-minute penalty. (5)

4) The only woman to ever play at the NHL level, Manon _____ (7)

5) Sweden, Finland & the Czech Republic won one of these at Turin, Italy. (5)

6) Person responsible for calling offsides. (8)

7) Before moving to Colorado, the Avalanche were the Quebec _____ (9)

8) These are handed out at the end of every game. (5)

9) "_____ Mario," Lemieux's nickname. (5)

10) Desjardins, Lindros, Brewer (4)

11) This call is negated if the goalie plays the puck. (5)

12) Wayne Gretzky had a record 92 of these in the 1981-82 season. (5)

13) The newest Canadian team, they joined the NHL in the 1992-93 season. (8)

 Through to 2006, 16 active NHL teams have won at least one Stanley Cup. How many can you name?

					2		
1							
				7			
		11					
	10				12		
6							3
			13				
	9				8		
	5					4	

Eleven women have had their names engraved on the Stanley Cup, including two team presidents, two team co-owners (Marian Ilitch, Detroit's co-owner, also included the names of her three daughters), one senior director of player's operations and two women in hockey operations.

Confused Names

The names of these young NHL stars have been mixed up.
See if you can put them back in the right order.

Sidney	Pitkanen
Dion	Nash
Alexander	Staal
Dany	Svatos
Joni	Heatley
Marek	Crosby
Michael	Ovechkin
Jason	Kovalchuk
Eric	Ryder
Rick	Spezza
Ales	Datsyuk
David	Hemsky
Ilya	Phaneuf
Pavel	Legwand

 Since the NHL implemented the best-of-seven Stanley Cup format in 1939, through to 2006, teams winning Game 1 of the finals have won the title: **A)** 47 percent of the time. **B)** 65 percent of the time. **C)** 79 percent of the time.

Family Matters

Match each family pair to their accomplishments in the hockey world by filling in the blank beside each name with either A or B.

1) Niedermayer

A) Before being joined by his brother in Anaheim, this center had two runs to the Stanley Cup final, one with the Mighty Ducks and one with the Florida Panthers.

B) This defenseman won the Norris trophy in 2003 for D-man of the year. He has won three Stanley Cups with the New Jersey Devils and a gold medal for Canada at the 2002 Olympics.

Rob: ___   Scott: ___

2) Hull

A) Finishing his career third on the all-time goal list with 741, he played in the All-Star game eight times and also won the Hart trophy for MVP during a career-high 86-goal season (third highest goal total ever recorded). He still holds the St. Louis Blues single-season records for goals and assists.

B) One of the first players to ever put a curve in his stick, this Hall of Famer's list of achievements includes winning the Hart trophy twice, being named to the NHL First All-Star team 10 times, winning the Cup twice and being the first player to ever record more than 50 goals in a season.

Brett: ___   Bobby: ___

3) Sutter

A) One of six Sutter brothers who made it to the NHL, he recorded 973 points in his 18-year career, winning the cup twice in the '80s with the Islanders. He later became the head coach of Canada's World Junior team, which won the gold medal at both the 2005 and 2006 championships.

B) After retiring from the NHL in 1986-87, he moved on to a successful career in coaching. Following stints as head coach of the San Jose Sharks and Chicago Blackhawks (where he played his entire NHL career), he became the head coach and GM of the Calgary Flames, leading them to the Stanley Cup finals in 2004.

Darryl: ___   Brent: ___

Only two teams, the 1942 Leafs and the 1975 Islanders, have ever come back from trailing a playoff series 3-0. The Leafs did it in the Stanley Cup final.

4) Lindros

A) Despite being drafted in the first round of the 1994 entry draft, he was forced to retire in 1996 after only 51 NHL games because of concussions. He moved on to host the *NHLPA Be A Player* television show, a weekly behind-the-scenes look at the hockey world.

B) Drafted by Quebec in 1991, this star refused to play for them and was traded to Philadelphia for six players, two first round draft picks and $15,000,000. As captain of the Flyers he won the Hart trophy as MVP in 1995 and led them to the Stanley Cup finals in 1997. He has played in six All-Star games and three Olympic games.

Brett: ___   Eric: ___

5) Bure

A) Nicknamed the Russian Rocket, he won Rookie of the Year in 1992 and helped the Vancouver Canucks reach the Cup finals in 1994. He led the league in goal scoring in 2000 and 2001 before being forced to retire in 2005 because of recurring knee injuries. After retirement he went on to become GM of the 2006 Russian Olympic team.

B) Married to Candace Cameron from *Full House*, he has spent time with Montreal, Calgary, Florida, St. Louis, Dallas and Los Angeles since joining the league in 1994. He has won a bronze medal in 2002 and a silver medal in 1998 with his brother on the Russian Olympic team.

Valeri: ___   Pavel: ___

6) Granato

A) The all-time leading scorer of the US National team, this player captained the team to the Gold medal at Nagano in 1998, while also carrying the flag at the opening ceremonies. After the Olympics, this star was hired by the L.A. Kings to do radio colour commentary, and has played in every World Championship for the USA. Granato also won a silver medal at the 2002 Olympics.

B) Drafted in 1982, this player has had a long and successful hockey career, including being named to the All-Rookie Team and, in 1997, winning the Bill Masterton trophy for perseverance and dedication to hockey. After retiring, Granato moved into the role of coaching, reaching the 50-win mark in only 87 games with the Avalanche, the 11th fastest among all-time NHL coaches.

Tony: ___   Cammi: ___

The Stanley Cup, first awarded in 1893, is North America's oldest professional sports trophy.

Word Work — Avalanche

See how many words you can make using only the letters in "Avalanche." They must be three letters or longer. Our crack team of wordsmiths at the Sports Puzzle Institute found 27. How many can you find? Here's the key:

0-5 words: Peewee player

6-10 words: Midget All-Star

11-15 words: AHL starter

16-20 words: NHL regular

21-27 words: Stanley Cup MVP

A V A L A N C H E

_____   _____   _____

_____   _____   _____

_____   _____   _____

_____   _____   _____

_____   _____   _____

_____   _____   _____

_____   _____   _____

_____   _____   _____

_____   _____   _____

_____   _____   _____

Best team ever? The 1955-56 Cup-winning Montreal Canadiens team lost only 17 games, and 11 players on the roster were later elected to the Hockey Hall of Fame.

Hidden Teams

Nine NHL team names are hidden below, starting with the central letter C and extending out. The letters can be connected on either side, above, below or diagonally. The same letter cannot be used twice in the same name. We've used either the first or last name of the team (i.e., Atlanta, or Thrashers).

I	O	U	A	R	O	K	S	Y
D	E	D	L	L	N	C	R	S
N	A	U	O	A	O	U	A	L
S	M	N	A	C	A	L	G	A
B	N	O	A	O	H	P	I	T
A	U	I	R	Y	O	I	A	G
S	B	L	O	T	E	S	C	O

The Montreal Canadiens led the league in scoring for 10 straight years, from 1953-54 to 1962-63. Not so coincidentally, they also won the Stanley Cup five years in a row, from 1956 to 1960.

A Little History

Circle which year these clues point towards.

1)
- Vincent Lecavalier, David Legwand and Brad Stuart are drafted first, second and third overall.
- The Detroit Red Wings sweep the Washington Capitals 4-0 to win the Stanley Cup.
- For the first time ever, women play ice hockey at the Olympics. Also for the first time, NHL players take part in the Games.

1990   1998   2002

2)
- The New Jersey Devils win the Cup by defeating Anaheim 4-3. Mighty Duck goalie J.S. Giguere is named the Playoff MVP.
- Marc-Andre Fleury, Eric Staal and Nathan Horton are drafted first, second and third.
- The Women's World Hockey Championship scheduled for Beijing, China, is cancelled due to the SARS outbreak.

1995   2001   2003

3)
- Gary Bettman takes over as Commissioner of the NHL. He changes the names of the conferences from "Campbell" and "Wales" to "Western" and "Eastern."
- The Florida Panthers and the Mighty Ducks of Anaheim join the NHL, making it a 26-team league.
- On the hundredth anniversary of the Stanley Cup, the Montreal Canadiens defeat the Los Angeles Kings 4-1.

1985   1988   1993

 How many Stanley Cups did Scotty Bowman win as a head coach? Also, in his 27-year coaching career, how many times did he finish the season with a losing record?

The Power Offs Puzzle

Enter a word in the centre that finishes the hockey expression on the left
and starts the one on the right.

Own	_____	Judge
Power	_____	Offs
Empty	_____	Minder
High	_____	Save
Give	_____	Game
Back	_____	Set
The Great	_____	Timer
Entry	_____	Pick
Minor	_____	Box
Over	_____	Out
Blue	_____	Change

In 2000, women's hockey was declared
an officially sanctioned NCAA championship
event. In the inaugural "Frozen Four,"
Minnesota-Duluth beat St. Lawrence 4-2.

Best of the Best

The last names of the top 18 all-time scorers in the NHL are hidden below.
They are written forwards or backwards, and are hidden diagonally, horizontally and
vertically. Watch out, the name of the 15th all-time point-getter is hidden twice. After you've
crossed out each name, the leftover letters spell out the 19th all-time top scorer, as of 2007.

S	A	K	I	C	O	F	F	E	Y
S	I	C	N	A	R	F	G	L	U
M	E	S	S	I	E	R	R	C	S
O	K	X	R	O	I	B	E	E	A
T	B	U	R	I	T	T	T	Y	T
I	O	E	H	U	T	A	Z	H	I
S	U	I	O	C	O	E	K	O	K
O	R	M	A	A	R	M	Y	W	I
P	Q	E	I	M	T	E	L	E	M
S	U	L	A	L	L	E	W	I	E
E	E	N	N	O	I	D	S	A	G
K	U	R	R	I	R	G	A	J	H

Names

Wayne GRETZKY
Mark MESSIER
Gordie HOWE
Ron FRANCIS
Marcel DIONNE
Steve YZERMAN
Mario LEMIEUX
Phil ESPOSITO
Ray BOURQUE

Paul COFFEY
Joe SAKIC
Jaromir JAGR
Stan MIKITA
Bryan TROTTIER
Adam OATES
Doug GILMOUR
Dale HAWERCHUK
Jari KURRI

During the lockout year, 388 NHLers played in European leagues. The most popular countries were Russia, with 78 players, Sweden, with 75 players, and the Czech Republic, with 51 players.

19th All-Time Scorer: __ __ __ __   __ __ __ __ __ __ __ __ __

Your Choice

See if you can pick the right answer.

1) **The Minnesota Wild are one of a kind in the NHL because ...**

   A) They are the only team that has never named a permanent captain. (They usually rotate captains every month.)
   B) They are the only team that does not end in the letter 'S'.
   C) Their players all wear matching Minnesota Wild boxers every game.
   D) For every home game they give away $1,000 to the fan who dances the wildest.

2) **What are the two most common jersey numbers of active players in the NHL (both shared by 22 players in 2006-07)?**

   A) 11 and 20
   B) 1 and 35
   C) 22 and 5
   D) 18 and 19

3) **What is the only jersey number never worn by a player in the NHL?**

   A) 84
   B) 0
   C) 61
   D) 73

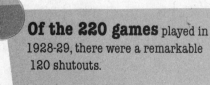

Of the 220 games played in 1928-29, there were a remarkable 120 shutouts.

4) **What is sometimes referred to as the "Gary Smith Rule"?**

   A) Coaches are not allowed to take a shift on the ice.
   B) A coach may not play more than one goalie at a time.
   C) Players on the ice may not wear headsets.
   D) Goalies cannot play the puck across centre.

5) **The largest crowd ever to watch a hockey game is 74,544. Where was it?**

   A) The opening game of the 2001 Central Collegiate Hockey Association's season between Michigan State University and the University of Michigan.
   B) "The Heritage Classic," an outdoor NHL game played between Edmonton and Montreal in 2003. The Canadiens won 4-3.
   C) The 2002 Women's Gold Medal game at the Olympics in Salt Lake City, between Canada and the USA.
   D) The final game of the 1972 Summit Series in Moscow, between Canada and the Soviet Union.

6) **Through to 2006, the Hart trophy for MVP has been awarded 82 times. Broken up by position, which one has won the most (44 times) and the least (four times)?**

   A) Centre most, defensemen least
   B) Right wing most, goalie least
   C) Defensemen most, right wing least
   D) Centre most, left wing least

7) What is the most common penalty in NHL history?

A) Roughing
B) Hooking
C) Interference
D) Fighting

8) What happened in Denver, Colorado, on November 9th, 1995?

A) Patrick Roy, arguably hockey's greatest goaltender, played his first game with the Avs.
B) The Avalanche sellout streak began. The longest of the four major leagues, they went on to sell out 487 straight games.
C) The Stanley Cup, while on display for the opening of Colorado's new arena, was stolen.
D) The game between Colorado and Boston was cancelled because both teams had been hit so badly by the flu that neither could ice a full squad.

9) Which strange feat did the Nashville Predators achieve in the 2005-06 season?

A) They had a better winning percentage when their opponents scored first (64 percent), than when the Preds did (57 percent).
B) They never scored more than 4 goals in a game.
C) They scored an NHL record 28 empty-net goals.
D) No player on the Preds recorded more than 50 points. (Paul Kariya had 49.)

10) From 1992-93 to 2003-04 (except for the Devils in 2000) only two teams led the NHL in shots in the regular season. Who were the two teams?

A) Pittsburgh and Colorado
B) Montreal and Dallas
C) Vancouver and Philadelphia
D) Detroit and Boston

 Lots of teams come and go in the NHL. Can you name the last five cities to lose a team, including those that moved to a new city? Extra credit if you can guess the last season they played.

What Did I Win?

Match the name of the trophy with what the award is given for.

Art Ross	Rookie of the Year
Bill Masterton	Best team in regular season
Calder	Coach of the Year
Conn Smythe	Regular season scoring champ
Frank J. Selke	Most outstanding goalie
Hart	Sportsmanship
Jack Adams	Playoff MVP
James Norris	Regular season MVP
Vezina	Top defensive forward
Maurice "Rocket" Richard	Most outstanding defenseman
Presidents' Trophy	Leader of the year
Mark Messier Award	Most goals in regular season

All-star goalie Ken Dryden never lost more than 10 games in a season during his eight-year career. He won the goalie of the year award five times.

Who Am I?

See if you can figure out who these clues point towards, in the fewest clues possible.

1

1) I appeared on *The Tonight Show* with Jay Leno on August 5, 2005.
2) When I was 15, Wayne Gretzky said I was "… the best player I've seen since Mario Lemieux." When I was 16, I became the youngest player to ever score a goal for Team Canada.
3) I chose my jersey number 87 because my birthday is August 7, 1987 (8/7/87).
4) In 2005, I was the first player drafted after the lockout, by Pittsburgh. That year I became the youngest player to register 100 points in an NHL season.

Who Am I? _____

2

1) In my final two years of Junior with the Prince Albert Raiders (WHL), I recorded an impressive 232 points in 106 games.
2) In 1988 I was drafted first overall, one of only five American-born players ever drafted first.
3) I am arguably the most decorated American player of all-time, including three appearances at the Olympics, two World Junior Championships, two World Cup of Hockey appearances and three World Championships.
4) I have been with the Dallas Stars since they moved from Minnesota, and in 2005 I signed a five-year contract to stay with the Stars. I hold team records for games played, goals, assists and points, and helped the team win its first Stanley Cup in 1999.

Who Am I? _____

 In 2006-07, there were 13 European captains in the NHL. How many can you name?

Kriss Kross

The player names below are listed according to their length.
Fit them into their proper place in the grid; there is only one correct place for each word.
We've started you off by filling in the name Staios – now find a six-letter name ending in 'T',
or a seven-letter name with 'I' as the fourth letter, etc. Good luck!

3 Letters
May
Orr
Roy

4 Letters
Hall
Klee
Mara
Nagy
Nash

5 Letters
Chara
Fahey
Gagne
Garon
Oliwa
Smyth
Suchy
Sydor
Young

6 Letters
Arnott
Crosby
Hejduk
Hrdina
Iginla
Joseph
Knuble
Staios
Thomas

7 Letters
Cassels
Gelinas
Grahame
Naslund
Simpson
St. Louis

8 Letters
Connolly

In 2005, the average weight of an NHL player was
204.9 lbs. In 1972, the average was 184.5 lbs.

In 2005, the average height of an NHL player was 6'1". In 1972, the average was 5'11".

Dream Arenas

Three of these NHL arena names are made up. See if you can spot them all.

Mellon Arena

Staples Center

Xcel Energy Center

Oreo Centre

St. Pete's Times Arena

American National Patriot Arena

Joe Louis Arena

United Center

HP Pavilion

McDonald's Place

The average NHL goalie wears around 50 pounds of equipment and sweats off between five to seven pounds each game.

Hidden Teams #2

Six NHL team names are hidden below, starting with the central letter B and extending out.
The letters can be connected on either side, above, below or diagonally.
The same letter cannot be used twice in the same name.
We've used either the first or last name of the team (i.e., Dallas, or Stars). Watch out,
one name is hidden twice.

S	N	O	H	K	C	E	N	O
K	W	A	T	A	U	F	S	L
T	S	S	L	L	U	I	F	C
E	W	T	O	B	L	A	O	S
S	K	K	R	L	U	A	L	K
N	C	U	U	K	C	F	W	O
M	I	A	J	E	H	A	K	T

 Which year were Roberto Luongo, Sergei
Samsonov and Brenden Morrow drafted? Who
was drafted first overall that year?

It's a Numbers Game

See if you can fill in the correct answer, choosing from numbers in the box below. Cross out each one as you go. This is one of the hardest puzzles in the book. Good luck!

1) Number of teams currently in the NHL

   _____

2) Total payroll of the 2003-04 Nashville Predators – lowest in the league

   _____

3) Total payroll of the 2003-04 Detroit Red Wings – highest in the league

   _____

4) Salary cap of the NHL in 2006-07 – the maximum salary any team could have

   _____

5) Fastest three goals scored by one player in a game – in seconds (held by Bill Mosienko)

   _____

6) Most NHL teams played for during a career (held by Mike Sillinger)

   _____

7) Number of Hart Trophies Wayne Gretzky won for league MVP in the 1980s

   _____

8) Average 2006-07 attendance at Montreal home games – highest in the league

   _____

9) Average 2006-07 attendance at St. Louis' home games – lowest in the league

   _____

There were 2,545 power-play goals in 2005-06, 464 more than in any previous year.

10) Total number of seasons played in the NHL, including 2007-08

_____

11) Minimum NHL player salary in 1963-64

_____

12) Highest salary ever paid to a player in the NHL (Jaromir Jagr)

_____

13) Average NHL player salary in 1990-01

_____

14) Average NHL player salary in 2003-04

_____

15) Most seasons played by one player in his career (held by Gordie Howe)

_____

16) Number of regular season games lost to the infamous lockout of 2004-05

_____

9	30	12,368	11,483,333
12	90	21,273	44,000,000
21	1,230	271,000	21,932,500
26	6,163	1,830,126	77,856,109

Most goalie masks are made out of Kevlar and fibreglass – the same materials used to make bulletproof vests.

Loony Lingo

Twelve common hockey terms have been mixed up. See if you can unscramble them all!

1) Lago Jegud   _____ _____

2) Tha Citrk   _____ _____

3) Torvmeei   _____

4) Grulera Asnose   _____ _____

5) Typelan   _____

6) Algreen Megaran   _____ _____

7) Veif Helo   _____ _____

8) Ryawbake   _____

9) Capbuk Alegoi   _____ _____

10) Fisenvoef Zeno   _____ _____

11) Bamonzi   _____

12) Odby Kehec   _____ _____

 Can you figure out what league each of these hockey teams play in? The Gwinnett Gladiators, the Montreal Axiom, the Hartford Wolf Pack, the Kelowna Rockets and the Omaha Ak-Sar-Ben Knights.

Know More Teams

See if you can identify which NHL team these clues point towards.

1) This team is a sub-species of puma.

   _____

2) You could name this team after someone like Brad Pitt, or even the Milky Way.

   _____

3) This team is named after part of a tree.

   _____

4) This team has been known to howl at the moon.

   _____

5) This team rules all.

   _____

6) This team is the most dangerous creature in the ocean.

   _____

7) This team can reach 50,000 degrees Fahrenheit!

   _____

8) This team is completely crazy and out of control.

   _____

9) The only team named after a bird … too bad the bird can't fly.

   _____

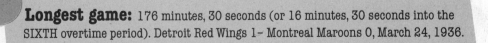

Longest game: 176 minutes, 30 seconds (or 16 minutes, 30 seconds into the SIXTH overtime period). Detroit Red Wings 1– Montreal Maroons 0, March 24, 1936.

Round and Round #2

This puzzle goes in a spiral, starting with the top left corner and working around until all the spaces are filled up. The start of the next clue is formed by the last one or two letters of the previous answer. The number in brackets at the end of each clue gives the number of letters in the answer. Try working backwards if you get stuck.

1) Type of cap (not the kind you wear). (6)

2) Montreal sniper Michael _____ (5)

3) Mike Keenan coached this team to a Cup in 1994. (7)

4) High - _____ (8)

5) G in GAA. (5)

6) Type of stick infraction. (8)

7) _____ Howe (6)

8) Conference (7)

9) Many players break this. (4)

10) Regular _____ (6)

11) Columbus sniper Rick _____ (4)

12) _____ - Handed (5)

13) John Tortorella coached this team to a Cup in 2004. (8)

From 1954 to 2006, there have been approximately 2,107,840 shots taken in regular season NHL games. That's a lot of rubber.

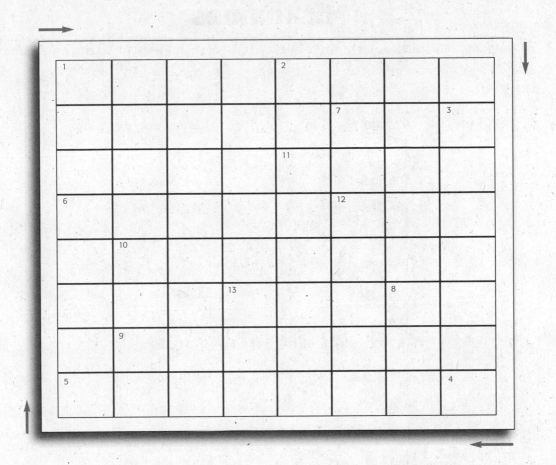

 Of the 42 NHLers selected for the 2007 All-Star Game, 20 were making their first appearance. How many of those All-Star rookies can you name?

Nicknames

Can you match the nicknames of these hockey stars, past and present, to their real names?

The Great One	Stu Grimson
Mr. Hockey	Teemu Selanne
The Russian Rocket	Bobby Hull
The Rocket	Dave Williams
The Dominator	Sidney Crosby
The Grim Reaper	Wayne Gretzky
The Kid	Pavel Bure
The Eagle	Ed Belfour
Tiger	Dominik Hasek
The Finnish Flash	Joe Sakic
The Flower	Nikolai Khabibulin
Burnaby Joe	Gordie Howe
Jovocop	Guy Lafleur
The Golden Jet	Maurice Richard
Bulin Wall	Ed Jovanovski

In 2005-06 Joe Thornton registered more assists (96) than the leading scorer from the previous season, Martin St. Louis, had in total points (94).

What Am I?

Try to figure out what these clues are pointing to, in as few clues as possible.

1

A) I used to have hard edges, now I'm smooth and rounded.

B) I'm 48 inches tall.

C) I have two pegs.

D) I can be both a goalie's best friend and a shooter's worst enemy.

What am I? _____

2

A) I originated, in my current form, around 1872.

B) I'm always kept frozen before big games.

C) I am one inch thick and three inches in diameter.

D) I am made of vulcanized rubber.

What am I? _____

Combined, the Montreal Canadiens and the Toronto Maple Leafs have won 37 Stanley Cups. The rest of the active NHL teams have won 45 total Cups, through 2007.

True or False

Can you figure out if each of the following is true or false? Circle your choice.

1) Art Ross, after whom the trophy for most points in a season is named, had only one point in his NHL career.

   True   **False**

2) The NHL ran a promotion on eBay in the summer of 2002, auctioning off one afternoon with the Stanley Cup. Adam Garrison, the winning bidder, paid $15,020 to spend four hours with the cup. He took it out for lunch and reportedly kissed it multiple times.

   True   **False**

3) At one point in the 2006-07 season, Carolina goalie Cam Ward was tied for the league-lead in points.

   True   **False**

4) In a 1947 World Hockey Championship game, Canada beat Denmark 47-0, and every Canadian except the goalie scored at least 3 goals.

   True   **False**

5) The Edmonton Oilers are the only team to record more than 100 shots in a game, taking an amazing 109 against the Buffalo Sabres in 1988. Edmonton won 8-3.

   True   **False**

6) Paul Kariya earned $10,000,000 per year from 1999 through 2003, with Anaheim. He took an $8.8 million pay-cut in 2003-04 to play with Colorado, at $1,200,000.

   True   **False**

 Which team has won the third-most Stanley Cups in NHL history? What about the fourth and fifth-most? Extra credit if you know the number of times each has won.

7) Jacques Demers, the only coach to win two Coach of the Year trophies in a row, is illiterate. (He can't read or write.)

True   **False**

8) From 1981 to 2001, only three different players led the NHL in points: Wayne Gretzky, Jaromir Jagr and Mario Lemieux

True   **False**

9) After retiring in 2003, Hall-of-Fame goalie Patrick Roy created a new fashion line, Essentials for Men.

True   **False**

10) After winning the Cup in 2001, Avalanche forward Shjon Podein wore his sweaty uniform, equipment and skates for more than 25 hours, even sleeping in his equipment. Why? It was a triple-dog dare.

True   **False**

11) Wayne Gretzky first appeared on the Hockey Night in Canada broadcast as a 10-year-old, interviewed between periods about his 378-goal Novice season.

True   **False**

12) The average salary of an NHL referee is higher than the average salary of an NHL coach.

True   **False**

From 1989 through to 2006, no team had lost in the Stanley Cup final twice. There were 17 different losing teams.

Kriss Kross #2

The player names below are listed according to their length. Fit them into their proper place in the grid; there is only one correct place for each word. We've started you off by filling in the name Auld – now find an eight-letter word ending in 'A', or a seven-letter word with 'L' as the third letter, and so on. Good luck!

4 Letters
Auld
Bonk
Dowd
Erat
Neil
Salo
Snow
Ward

5 Letters
Drury
Grier
Koivu
Satan
Staal
Turco
White

6 Letters
Arnott
Bondra
Briere
Dvorak
Frolov
Kvasha
Madden
Markov
Redden
Stajan
Vrbata

7 Letters
Dingman
Nabokov
Ribeiro
Roenick
Rolston
Svoboda

8 Letters
Cheechoo
Niinimaa
Nylander
Raycroft

The Edmonton Oilers
are the only eighth-seeded team to make it to the Stanley Cup finals, losing to Carolina in 2005-06.

 Ten players in NHL history have received eight-digit salaries, signing bonuses included. How many can you name?

Wacky Names

There have been some weird names in the history of the NHL.
See if you can spot the four made-up names from the list of past and current players below.

Turk Broda   Max Short

Fred Saskamoose   Hakan Loob

Fedor Fedorov   Kimmo Timmonen

Mario Marois   Derek Boogaard

Viktor Von Ross   Frank McCool

Butch Goring   Darren Puppa

Per-Olav Brasar   Igor Gorbgorbov

Tuomo Ruutu   Jordin Tootoo

Ebenezer R. Goodfellow   Peter Puck

After winning the Cup in 1984, Edmonton owner
Peter Pocklington submitted the list of names to be inscribed
on the Cup. He included his father, Basil, who had nothing
to do with the team. After discovering this, the NHL had
his inscription replaced with a line of 16 Xs.

Hidden Teams #3

Six NHL team names are hidden below, starting with the central letter P and extending out. The letters can be connected on either side, above, below or diagonally. The same letter cannot be used twice in the same name. We've used either the first or last name of the team (i.e., Edmonton, or Oilers). Watch out, one name is hidden twice!

H	P	T	E	P	A	L	S	R
I	H	L	N	D	I	T	O	A
A	X	E	A	H	R	E	A	S
X	R	N	R	P	E	N	D	N
S	I	T	A	H	I	G	I	H
S	H	N	O	T	O	U	B	G
R	E	X	E	N	T	S	U	R

Through the first eight women's World Hockey Championship tournaments (1990, '92, '94, '97, '99, 2000, '01, and '04), Canada won gold every time. In 2005, the United States, eight-time runner-up, finally took the gold.

What's in a Name?

We took the rosters of the last 20 Stanley Cup-winning teams to see what the most common first names were. Each clue lists three players; you must figure out which first name they share. The number in brackets represents the number of Cup winners with that name; repeated winners don't count more than once. Don't worry if your own name isn't very common; there have also been an Esa, a Reijo and a Gaston hoisting the Cup.

#1) _____ Richter, Ricci, Modano (16)

#2) _____ Dingman, Osgood, Simon (8)

#3) _____ Duchesne, Smith, Yzerman (7)

#4) _____ Gelinas, Cibak, Gerber (7)

#5) _____ Gionta, Rolston, Rafalski (6)

#6) _____ MacTavish, Adams, Ludwig (6)

#7) _____ Andreychuk, Reid, Hannan (6)

#8) _____ Mullen, Kocur, Sakic (5)

#9) _____ Stevens, Gomez, Niedermayer (5)

#10) _____ Weight, Lidster, Gilmour (5)

The Buffalo Sabres opened the 2006-07 season 10-0, tied with the '93 Leafs as the best opening record in NHL history.

Word Work – Detroit

See how many words you can make using only the letters in "Detroit." They must be three letters or longer. Our crack team of wordsmiths at the Sports Puzzle Institute found 37. How many can you find? Here's the key:

0-10 words: Bantam player   10-20 words: AHL starter

20-30 words: NHL regular   30-36 words: Stanley Cup MVP

DETROIT

_____   _____   _____

_____   _____   _____

_____   _____   _____

_____   _____   _____

_____   _____   _____

_____   _____   _____

_____   _____   _____

_____   _____   _____

_____   _____   _____

 In which year were Marian Gaborik, Dany Heatley and Ilja Bryzgalov drafted? Who was drafted first overall that year?

World-Class Word Search

The last names of 18 world-class women's hockey players are hidden below. They are written forwards or backwards, and are hidden diagonally, horizontally and vertically. After you've crossed out each name, the leftover letters will spell out the top scorer at the 2006 Winter Olympics.

T	H	D	R	O	F	F	E	H	R
A	R	Y	L	E	E	G	Y	L	E
L	U	E	S	W	P	N	L	I	S
E	G	H	F	S	C	I	K	S	I
H	G	E	C	I	R	K	P	U	E
M	I	N	H	E	L	A	E	N	H
A	E	M	T	S	L	O	H	O	N
N	R	T	A	P	P	S	V	H	E
N	O	S	S	R	E	D	N	A	K
B	I	P	O	T	T	E	R	R	C
R	E	S	A	K	S	I	E	A	I
P	E	H	K	O	N	E	N	R	W

Top Olympic Scorer:

___ ___ ___ ___ ___ ___ ___   ___ ___ ___ ___ ___ ___ ___ ___ ___

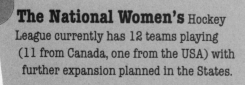

The National Women's Hockey League currently has 12 teams playing (11 from Canada, one from the USA) with further expansion planned in the States.

Names

Gunilla ANDERSSON
Jennifer BOTTERILL
Jennifer HARSS
Erika HOLST
Katie KING
Kim MARTIN
Cherie PIPER
Angela RUGGIERO
Svetlana TREFILOVA

Gillian APPS
Julie CHU
Jayna HEFFORD
Waltraud KASER
Kathrin LEHMANN
Mari PEHKONEN
Jenny POTTER
Vicky SUNOHARA
Hayley WICKENHEISER

Who Am I? #2

See if you can figure out who these clues point towards, in the fewest clues possible.

1

1) I was born in Cranbrook, British Columbia. My middle name is Gregory.
2) In my 22-year career I stayed with the team that drafted me in 1983, making the playoffs an amazing 20 times.
3) I retired in the summer of 2006 as the longest-serving captain in the history of the NHL, at 20 years. In that time, I led my team to the Stanley Cup in 1997, 1998 and 2002.
4) In 1,514 regular-season games with Detroit, I had 1,755 points, sixth all-time in NHL scoring. I have won the Lester B. Pearson, Frank J. Selke, Conn Smythe and Bill Masterton trophies.

Who Am I? _____

2

1) I have never seen a Stanley Cup game, but I was inducted to the Hockey Hall of Fame in 1945.
2) I returned to England in 1893, where I became the Lord Mayor of Liverpool.
3) As the Governor General of Canada, I donated one of the most coveted trophies in professional sports.
4) The first clue contains half the answer.

Who Am I? _____

 Which player has won the most Stanley Cups in NHL history? Who has won the second and third most?

Odd One Out

Can you answer all of these questions? Make sure you read them carefully.

1) Which one of these players does not have a brother who also played in the NHL?

A) Sergei Fedorov
B) Wayne Gretzky
C) Jaromir Jagr
D) Mark Messier

2) Which of the following was never a part of the NHL rules?

A) The goal judge was required to stand on the ice behind the net.
B) The Mercy Rule: If one team was losing by more than eight goals, the game would automatically end (to avoid excessive fighting).
C) Goalies were penalized if they fell to the ice to make a save. They were given a warning the first time, then a penalty and a $2 fine.
D) Players used to have to shoot from behind a line 38 feet from the goal when taking penalty shots; they could not deke in on the goalie.

3) Which of the following facts about Wayne Gretzky is not true?

A) Despite winning the Hart and Lady Byng trophies in his first year in the NHL, Gretzky did not win the Calder for Rookie of the Year.
B) His full name is Wayne Maximus Gretzky.
C) Gretzky has more assists (1,963) than any other player has points.
D) On his 18th birthday, Gretzky signed a 21-year WHA contract with the Edmonton Oilers.

4) Which of the following things never happened to the Stanley Cup?

A) Martin Brodeur took it to a movie theatre and ate popcorn out of it.
B) Brad Richards wore it on his back while jet skiing. The Cup even had its own life jacket.
C) Sylvain Lefebvre had his daughter baptized in it.
D) In 1927, wild man Willie Barner went over Niagara Falls in a barrel with Lord Stanley's Cup. Both survived with small bumps & bruises. (There is still a small dent in the Cup today.)

The most shots ever recorded by one team in one game is 83, by the Boston Bruins in 1941. They beat Chicago, but only by a score of 3-2.

5) **Which of the following teams has never won the Cup?**

A) Los Angeles Kings
B) Pittsburgh Penguins
C) New York Rangers
D) Calgary Flames

6) **Which of the following things did the New York Islanders not do?**

A) Fire their General Manager 40 days after hiring him. In replacement, they hired their backup goalie from the 2005-06 season, Garth Snow.
B) Sign Alexei Yashin to a 10-year, $87 million US contract, the largest deal in NHL history.
C) Sign goalie Rick DiPietro to a 15-year, $67.5 million US contract, the longest deal in NHL history.
D) Trade their first-round pick in the NHL Entry Draft four years in a row. They have not had a first-round pick since 2002.

7) **Which of the following countries has never won an Olympic hockey medal, men's or women's?**

A) Great Britain
B) Switzerland
C) Japan
D) Finland

8) **Which of the following was not an Original Six NHL team?**

A) Boston Bruins
B) Philadelphia Flyers
C) Toronto Maple Leafs
D) Chicago Blackhawks

9) **Which of the following facts about Gordie Howe is not true?**

A) Howe played in the All-Star game 23 times.
B) Howe is the only player to compete in professional hockey in five different decades (1940s through 1980s). He retired at age 52.
C) Late in his career, Howe played on the same team as his two sons, Mark and Marty.
D) In 1984, Canadian Prime Minister Brian Mulroney named Howe the honorary Minister of Sports, a position he held for 12 years.

In 1917 there were only seven players on each team, and back then an extra seventh skater (the rover) was always on the ice, so players skated a full 60 minutes every game.

Post-Season Crozzle

Fill in the crossword grid by answering each clue, corresponding to the number in the grid.

Across

4) _____ Forsberg
7) Three goals
9) One of the lines on the ice
10) Defensive strategy
11) ____ - shot
14) Russian prodigy Evgeni _____
15) Way to acquire a new player
18) Joined NHL in 2000
20) Three NHL teams start with this
22) A team with a 10 – 0 record

Down

1) No goals
2) Joined NHL in 1999
3) One of the greatest defensemen ever
4) Abbreviation for having one man in the box
5) Leafs team, short form
6) Team known for octopi on the ice
8) Joined NHL same time as 18 across
12) Coach may do this to his goalie
13) Playoff insult: "Don't miss your ____ time!"
16) _____ Alfredsson
17) Type of illegal pass
18) Too many _____
19) _____ strength
21) Capitals team, short form
22) ___ - stairs
23) Lightning team, short form

From 1954 to 2006, there have been approximately 1,211,341 total penalty minutes, an average of 34 PIM per game. Taken at once, that's almost two and a half years in the sin bin!

 In 1970, Bobby Orr became the first defenseman to win this award. Can you name it, along with the other four trophies he won that year?

Lost Letters #2

Fill in the missing letter in the middle to complete the last letter of the player's name on the left, and the first letter of the name on the right. The missing letters, taken from top to bottom, spell out the name of the first player ever drafted in the inaugural Entry Draft of 1963.

Henrik Zetterber	___	rant Marshall
Paul Mar	___	ntti Laaksonen
J.P. Vigie	___	ick Nash
Colton Or	___	adek Bonk
Marc-Andre Fleur	___	ann Danis
Clarke Wil	___	arek Malik
Mike Modan	___	lli Jokinen
Serge Aubi	___	ikolai Zherdev
Rico Fat	___	les Kotalik
Curtis Josep	___	annu Toivonen
Martin Strak	___	aron Johnson
Mats Sundi	___	ils Ekman

First player ever drafted in the NHL:

_____

From 1954 to 2006, there have been a total of 226,902 goals in 35,273 total regular season NHL games, an average of 6.4 goals per game. Stacked on top of each other, all those pucks would be almost six kilometres high!

The World's Game

Roberto Luongo	-	Canada
Brian Rafalski	-	USA
Fredrik Modin	-	Sweden
Pavel Datsyuk	-	Russia
Milan Hejduk	-	Czech Republic
Katie King	-	USA
Marco Sturm	-	Germany
Sandis Ozolinsh	-	Latvia
Marian Gaborik	-	Slovakia
David Aebischer	-	Switzerland
Nikolai Antropov	-	Kazakhstan
Sarah Vaillancourt	-	Canada
Miikka Kiprusoff	-	Finland

Beginner's Luck

T	R	S	A	M	S	O	N	O	V
N	U	R	E	T	U	S	V	R	O
H	O	D	R	A	R	E	B	A	K
E	F	S	R	O	C	N	T	Y	V
A	L	O	S	H	M	H	D	C	O
T	E	A	K	D	C	N	P	R	K
L	B	I	R	T	E	L	E	O	O
E	N	U	E	W	G	R	L	F	B
Y	R	E	U	O	E	A	F	T	A
Y	L	E	M	I	E	U	X	L	N
F	I	E	N	N	A	L	E	S	A
N	Z	J	A	C	K	M	A	N	S

The leftover letters spell out Toronto Maple Leafs.

Famous Firsts

1	–	C
2	–	B
3	–	A
4	–	D
5	–	B
6	–	A
7	–	A
8	–	D
9	–	B

Dream Teams

Winnipeg Winners
Buffalo Buffaloes
Kansas City Cavaliers

Q Answer: The 1992-93 San Jose Sharks lost a record 71 games, finishing 11-71-2.

Lost Letters

Steve Poaps	_T_	odd Marchant
Carlo Colaiacov	_O_	laf Kolzig
Joe Thornto	_N_	iklas Lidstrom
Chris Drur	_Y_	an Stasny
Gilbert Brul	_E_	rik Cole
Andrej Meszaro	_S_	ean O'Donnell
Wayne Van Dor	_P_	avel Vorobiev
Marty Turc	_O_	le-Kristian Tollefsen
Brad Boye	_S_	ami Salo
Matthew Lombard	_I_	an Moran
Martin Era	_T_	om Poti
Mike Ribeir	_O_	ssi Vaananen

The (Inter) National Hockey League

#1)	Canada
#2)	USA
#3)	Czech Republic
#4)	Russia
#5)	Sweden
#6)	Finland
#7)	Slovakia
#8)	Germany
#9)	Ukraine
#10)	Switzerland

Note: Ukraine and Switzerland are tied with five players in the NHL.

Game Day Crozzle

Across

1) Shootout
5) Man
8) Match
9) Blueline
11) USA
13) Left wing
15) Cash
16) Empty
18) Tied
19) Co
20) Kurri
21) Ice

Down

2) Hall
3) Oilers
4) Time out
5) Mats
6) NWHL
7) Tip
9) Bodycheck
10) Son
11) Upset
12) Al
14) Goalie
16) Ed
17) Puck

Q Answer: Teemu Selanne, 1999 • Pavel Bure, 2000 • Pavel Bure, 2001 • Jarome Iginla, 2002 • Milan Hejduk, 2003 • Rick Nash, Ilya Kovalchuk, Jarome Iginla, 2004 • Jonathan Cheechoo, 2006

Fill Me In

1A) Even Strength
1B) Power Play
1C) Short-Handed
1D) Penalty Shot
1E) Empty-Net

2A) Tampa Bay Lightning
2B) New Jersey Devils
2C) Detroit Red Wings
2D) Colorado Avalanche
2E) New Jersey Devils

The leftover letters spell Mario Lemieux, the only player to score every type of goal in a single game.

Know Your Teams

1) Ottawa Senators
2) St. Louis Blues
3) Colorado Avalanche
4) New Jersey Devils
5) Calgary Flames
6) Carolina Hurricanes
7) Montreal Canadiens
8) Anaheim Ducks
9) Buffalo Sabres

Q Answer: Terry Sawchuk holds the record with 103 career shutouts. George Hainsworth is second, with 94, and Martin Brodeur is third with 92.

What Do They Have in Common?

1) A
2) B
3) B
4) C
5) C
6) D
7) A
8) B
9) B
10) A

Round and Round

1) Bettman
2) Anaheim
3) Minor
4) Rheaume
5) Medal
6) Linesman
7) Nordiques
8) Stars
9) Super
10) Eric
11) Icing
12) Goals
13) Senators

Q Answer: Boston Bruins, Calgary Flames, Carolina Hurricanes, Colorado Avalanche, Chicago Blackhawks, Dallas Stars, Detroit Red Wings, Edmonton Oilers, Montreal Canadiens, New Jersey Devils, New York Islanders, New York Rangers, Philadelphia Flyers, Pittsburgh Penguins, Tampa Bay Lightning, Toronto Maple Leafs

Confused Names

Sidney Crosby
Dion Phaneuf
Alexander Ovechkin
Dany Heatley
Joni Pitkanen
Marek Svatos
Michael Ryder
Jason Spezza
Eric Staal
Rick Nash
Ales Hemsky
David Legwand
Ilya Kovalchuk
Pavel Datsyuk

Q Answer: C) 79 percent of the time.

Family Matters

1) Rob **A** – Scott **B**
2) Brett **A** – Bobby **B**
3) Darryl **B** – Brent **A**
4) Brett **A** – Eric **B**
5) Valeri **B** – Pavel **A**
6) Tony **B** – Cammi **A**

ANSWERS

Word Work – Avalanche

Ace	Hen
Ache	Lace
Ale	Lance
Ave	Lane
Can	Lava
Canal	Leach
Cane	Lean
Cave	Naval
Clan	Nave
Clean	Navel
Each	Valance
Halve	Van
Have	Vane
Haven	Veal
Heal	Venal

Hidden Teams

Teams: Calgary, Canadiens, Canucks, Capitals, Carolina, Chicago, Colorado, Columbus, Coyotes.

A Little History

1) 1998
2) 2003
3) 1993

Q Answer: Scotty Bowman won nine Stanley Cups, and has never coached an NHL team with a losing record.

The Power Offs Puzzle

Goal
Play
Net
Stick
Away
Up
One
Draft
Penalty
Time
Line

Best of the Best

Note: Oates is hidden twice in the puzzle.

The leftover letters spell out Luc Robitaille, 19th all-time scoring leader.

Your Choice

1 - A
2 - A
3 - A
4 - D (Gary Smith, a goalie who played in the '60s and '70s, used to skate up the ice and stand in front of the opposing team's goalie.)
5 - A
6 - D
7 - B
8 - B
9 - A
10 - D

Q Answer: Hartford Whalers, 1997 (moved to Carolina). Winnipeg Jets, 1996 (moved to Phoenix). Quebec Nordiques, 1995 (moved to Colorado). Minnesota North Stars, 1993 (moved to Dallas). Colorado Rockies, 1982 (moved to New Jersey).

What Did I Win?

- Art Ross – Regular season scoring champ
- Bill Masterton – Sportsmanship
- Calder – Rookie of the Year
- Conn Smythe – Playoff MVP
- Frank J. Selke – Top defensive forward
- Hart – Regular season MVP
- Jack Adams – Coach of the Year
- James Norris – Most outstanding defenseman
- Vezina – Most outstanding goalie
- Maurice "Rocket" Richard – Most goals in regular season
- Presidents' Trophy – Best team in regular season (most points)
- Mark Messier Award – Leader of the year

Who Am I?

1 – Sidney Crosby
2 – Mike Modano

Q Answer: Markus Naslund, Mats Sundin, Kimmo Timonen, Peter Forsberg, Patrick Elias, Nicklas Lidstrom, Zdeno Chara, Jaromir Jagr, Daniel Alfredsson, Saku Koivu, Alexei Yashin, Olli Jokinen and Mattias Norstrom.

Kriss Kross

S	T	L	O	U	I	S			H	E	J	D	U	K
U			R		M	A	R	A		O				N
C	H	A	R	A		Y		L		S				U
H			T		K	L	E	E		E				B
Y	O	U	N	G		H		P						L
	L		A				G	R	A	H	A	M	E	
	I		I	G	I	N	L	A		R		A		
	W		N		A		A	R		N	A	G	Y	
C	A	S	S	E	L	S		O		O		E		N
	I				S	H		N		T		L		A
T	H	O	M	A	S		F		S	T	A	I	O	S
	P				A	Y		Y		N				L
C	R	O	S	B	Y		H	R	D	I	N	A		U
	O				E		E		O			S		N
C	O	N	N	O	L	L	Y		R	O	Y			D

Dream Arenas

Oreo Centre
American National Patriot Arena
McDonald's Place

Hidden Teams #2

Note: Blackhawks is hidden twice.

Teams: Blackhawks, Blue Jackets, Blues, Boston, Buffalo.

Q Answer: The year was 1997, and Joe Thornton was drafted first by the Bruins.

It's a Numbers Game

1)	30	9)	12,368
2)	21,932,500	10)	90
3)	77,856,109	11)	6,163
4)	44,000,000	12)	11,483,333
5)	21	13)	271,000
6)	12	14)	1,830,126
7)	9	15)	26
8)	21,273	16)	1,230

Loony Lingo

1)	Goal Judge	7)	Five Hole
2)	Hat Trick	8)	Breakaway
3)	Overtime	9)	Backup Goalie
4)	Regular Season	10)	Offensive Zone
5)	Penalty	11)	Zamboni
6)	General Manager	12)	Body Check

Answer: Gwinnett Gladiators: ECHL • Montreal Axiom: NWHL • Hartford Wolf Pack: AHL • Kelowna Rockets: WHL (major junior) • Omaha Ak-Sar-Ben Knights: AHL.

Know More Teams

1) Florida Panthers
2) Dallas Stars
3) Toronto Maple Leafs
4) Phoenix Coyotes
5) Los Angeles Kings
6) San Jose Sharks
7) Tampa Bay Lightning
8) Minnesota Wild
9) Pittsburgh Penguins

Round and Round #2

1) Salary
2) Ryder
3) Rangers
4) Sticking
5) Goals
6) Slashing
7) Gordie
8) Eastern
9) Nose
10) Season
11) Nash
12) Short
13) Tampa Bay

Q Answer: Ryan Miller, Cristobal Huet, Brian Campbell, Jay Bouwmeester, Sidney Crosby, Alexander Ovechkin, Daniel Briere, Jason Blake, Eric Staal, Justin Williams, Miikka Kiprusoff, Philippe Boucher, Dion Phaneuf, Lubomir Visnovsky, Jonathan Cheechoo, Martin Havlat, Andy McDonald, Yanic Perreault, Brian Rolston, Ryan Smith.

Nicknames

The Great One	–	Wayne Gretzky
Mr. Hockey	–	Gordie Howe
The Russian Rocket	–	Pavel Bure
The Rocket	–	Maurice Richard
The Dominator	–	Dominik Hasek
The Grim Reaper	–	Stu Grimson
The Kid	–	Sidney Crosby
The Eagle	–	Ed Belfour
Tiger	–	Dave Williams
The Finnish Flash	–	Teemu Selanne
The Flower	–	Guy Lafleur
Burnaby Joe	–	Joe Sakic
Jovocop	–	Ed Jovanovski
The Golden Jet	–	Bobby Hull
Bulin Wall	–	Nikolai Khabibulin

What Am I?

1 – Goal posts
2 – Hockey puck

True or False

1	–	True	7 –	True
2	–	False	8 –	True
3	–	True	9 –	False
4	–	True	10 –	True
5	–	False	11 –	True
6	–	True	12 –	False

Q Answer: The Detroit Red Wings are third with 10 Cups. The Edmonton Oilers and Boston Bruins are tied for fourth with five Cups each.

Kriss Kross #2

```
N I I N I M A A     S A L O         F
Y   E   A   U   A             G R I E R
L   I   I   R O L S T O N         O     A
A   L   O         D A       B     L O V Y
N   O         N A B O K O V       V     C
D   K O I V U     D V O R A K   S       R
E   V   D         R       O     V       O
R   A   D         U       E A R N O T T F
    S N O W       R       E     B       T
    H   W         Y   R I B E I R O     S
W A R D           C               N     T
H               T   K   V R B A T A     A
D I N G M A N   U           O     N     J
  I             D       B R I E R E     A
  T             D           R E D D E N
  E             C               A
C H E E C H O O                 R
                        S T A A L
```

Q Answer: Pavel Bure, Sergei Federov, Peter Forsberg, Chris Gratton, Jaromir Jagr, Paul Kariya, Mario Lemieux, Nicklas Lidstrom, Joe Sakic and Keith Tkachuk.

Wacky Names

- Max Short
- Igor Gorbgorbov
- Viktor Von Ross
- Peter Puck

Hidden Teams #3

Note: Panthers is hidden twice.

Teams: Panthers, Predators, Pittsburgh, Penguins, Philadelphia, Phoenix.

What's in a Name?

1) Mike
2) Chris
3) Steve
4) Martin
5) Brian
6) Craig
7) Dave
8) Joe
9) Scott
10) Doug

Word Work – Detroit

Doe	Rod
Die	Rode
Diet	Roe
Dot	Rot
Dote	Rotted
Dire	Tide
Dirt	Tie
Ditto	Tied
Ire	Tire
Ode	Tired
Ore	Toe
Red	Tore
Redo	Tort
Retort	Tote
Retro	Tried
Rid	Trio
Ride	Trite
Riot	Trot
Rite	

Answer: The year was 2000, and Rick DiPietro was drafted first overall by the Islanders.

World-Class Wordsearch

The leftover letters spell Hayley Wickenheiser, top scorer at the 2006 Olympics.

Who Am I? #2

1 – Steve Yzerman
2 – Lord Stanley, Earl of Preston

Answer: Henri Richard has won the most, with 11. Jean Beliveau and Yvan Cournoyer are tied for second, with 10.

Odd One Out

1) C
2) B
3) B – (His full name is Wayne Douglas Gretzky.)
4) D
5) A
6) D
7) C – (Switzerland won bronze in 1928 and 1948. Great Britain won bronze in 1924.)
8) B
9) D

Post-Season Crozzle

Across
4) Peter
7) Hat Trick
9) Red
10) Trap
11) Slap
14) Malkin
15) Trade
18) Minnesota
20) New
22) Undefeated

Down
1) Shutout
2) Atlanta
3) Orr
4) PK
5) TOR
6) Red Wings
8) Columbus
12) Pull
13) Tee
16) Daniel
17) Hand
18) Men
19) Even
21) WAS
22) Up
23) TB

Answer: In 1970, Bobby Orr won the Art Ross, Conn Smythe, Norris and Hart Trophies, as well as the Stanley Cup. He was the first D-Man to ever win the Art Ross, a feat he repeated in 1975.

Lost Letters #2

Henrik Zetterber	_G_	rant Marshall
Paul Mar	_A_	ntti Laaksonen
J.P. Vigie	_R_	ick Nash
Colton Or	_R_	adek Bonk
Marc-Andre Fleur	_Y_	ann Danis
Clarke Wil	_M_	arek Malik
Mike Modan	_O_	lli Jokinen
Serge Aubi	_N_	ikolai Zherdev
Rico Fat	_A_	les Kotalik
Curtis Josep	_H_	annu Toivonen
Martin Strak	_A_	aron Johnson
Mats Sundi	_N_	ils Ekman